Mountaineering Adventures

by Matt Doeden

Consultants:
John and Maggie Owen
American Alpine Club Library

CAPSTONE BOOKS

an imprint of Capstone Press
Mankato, Minnesota

Capstone Books are published by Capstone Press
151 Good Counsel Drive, P.O. Box 669, Mankato, Minnesota 56002
http://www.capstone-press.com

Library of Congress Cataloging-in-Publication Data
Doeden, Matt.
  Mountaineering adventures/by Matt Doeden.
  p. cm.—(Dangerous adventures)
  Includes bibliographical references (p. 45) and index.
  Summary: Describes mountain climbing, its history, equipment, and dangers, and some climbers' adventures.
  ISBN 0-7368-0575-3
  1. Mountaineering—Juvenile literature. [1. Mountaineering.] I. Title. II. Series.
GV200 .D64 2001
796.52'2—dc21   00-027216

Editorial Credits
Carrie A. Braulick, editor; Heather Kindseth, cover designer and illustrator;
  Katy Kudela and Jodi Theisen, photo researchers

Photo Credits
Archive Photos, 10, 12, 19, 20, 35, 36; Archive Photos/Wolfgang Rattay, 26
Index Stock Imagery, 7, 14, 32, 38
International Stock/Brent Winebrenner, 4; Esben Hardt, 42
Jack Olson, 29
James Kay/Pictor, 9, 24
Junko Tabei, 23
Northwind Picture Archives, 16
Photri-Microstock, 44; Photri-Microstock/Bannock, cover

1 2 3 4 5 6 06 05 04 03 02 01

Table of Contents

Chapter 1

Mountain Climbing

On May 29, 1953, Edmund Hillary and Tenzing Norgay stood about 1,000 feet (300 meters) below the summit of Mount Everest. They were near the highest point of the world's tallest mountain. Mount Everest is located between the Asian country of Nepal and the Tibet region of China.

No one had ever reached Mount Everest's highest point. Hillary and Norgay used bottled oxygen to help them breathe at this high altitude. Their bottles were running low of the gas.

Hillary and Norgay did not turn back. They reached the summit and stood 29,028 feet (8,848 meters) above the surface of the ocean.

Mount Everest is the world's tallest mountain.

Newspapers around the world included stories about their successful climb.

Expeditions

Mountain climbers also are called mountaineers. They go on mountain climbing expeditions. Expeditions can last several months. Mountain climbers usually are members of expedition teams. Expedition team members can help other team members who become sick or injured. Teams may include as few as two members. Some expedition teams include more than 50 people.

Mountain climbers go on expeditions for a variety of reasons. Some climb for recreation. Others climb to perform scientific research. For example, they may study plants and animals that live in mountainous areas. They may climb to take measurements of a mountain's height. Climbers also may want to take photographs or gather information to write books.

Camps

Mountain climbers stay at camps during long expeditions. They set up tents and unpack supplies at camps. They often cook food at their camps.

Mountain climbers set up tents and unpack supplies at camps.

Climbers sometimes set up camps at certain areas on a mountain. Mount Everest has five of these established areas. Climbers have used these areas for more than 40 years. Mount Everest's main camping area is called base camp. It is located 17,500 feet (5,334 meters) up the mountain.

Climbers often rest at camps. They let their bodies become used to high altitudes. The air contains little oxygen at altitudes of about 8,000 feet (2,400 meters) or higher. People who climb too quickly at these altitudes may get altitude sickness. Climbers sometimes call this condition mountain sickness. Climbers who suffer from altitude sickness may have cramps, headaches, and difficulty breathing. They often tire easily. Climbers sometimes carry oxygen tanks to prevent altitude sickness. They also climb slowly and rest often.

Climbing Dangers

Mountain climbers face many dangers. Hypothermia is one of the most common and deadly dangers. This condition occurs when a person's body temperature becomes too low. The air at high altitudes is colder than air at lower altitudes. Climbers' bodies sometimes cannot produce enough energy to stay warm.

Climbers try to prevent hypothermia. They wear layers of warm, waterproof clothing. They also wear light clothing. This helps climbers move more comfortably. Climbers also eat high-energy food such as peanut butter

Mountain climbers must dress warmly to prevent hypothermia.

sandwiches and nuts. These foods give climbers extra energy that helps them withstand cold temperatures.

Climbers also may suffer from frostbite. This condition occurs when cold temperatures cause the skin to freeze. Climbers' outside layer of clothing often is waterproof. It is important that climbers' skin remains dry. Wet skin freezes more quickly than dry skin does.

Mountain climbers use equipment such as ropes and harnesses to help them climb.

Climbers need to protect themselves from sunburn. The sun's rays are more powerful at high altitudes. The air at these altitudes contains little oxygen and other chemicals. This thin air cannot absorb the sun's rays. Sun rays also reflect off snow and ice. Climbers wear sunblock lotion to prevent sunburn.

Climbers may become snowblind. This painful condition occurs when sun rays that reflect off snow and ice cause climbers' eyes to become irritated. Climbers wear tinted goggles or sunglasses to prevent snowblindness.

Avalanches and severe weather also are dangerous to climbers. Avalanches occur when large amounts of snow, ice, or earth become loose and slide down mountainsides. Avalanches can bury climbers or block climbers' paths. Severe weather may include strong winds and snowfall. Strong winds can cause climbers to fall. Snow can prevent climbers from seeing where they are going. These climbers may become lost.

Equipment

Climbers use a variety of equipment. This equipment must be strong. Equipment failures can place climbers' lives in danger. Ropes and harnesses are made of nylon. This strong material does not break easily. Climbers wear ropes attached to harnesses to protect them from falls. Harnesses have leg loops and a waist belt.

Crampons are one of climbers' most important pieces of equipment. Crampons are sharp metal spikes that help climbers gain footholds on icy and snowy surfaces. Straps attach crampons to the bottom of climbers' boots.

Climbers sometimes use ice axes. Ice axes have long, curved blades with teeth. Climbers push the axes into ice or snow. They often use ice axes to stop themselves from falling.

Climbers may use a variety of anchors to hold ropes in place. They sometimes hammer long metal spikes called pitons into mountain surfaces. They may use deadman anchors on snowy surfaces. A cable runs through the middle of these metal plates. To use deadman anchors, climbers first create an opening in the snow with an ice axe. They then hammer the plate into the opening and attach their rope to the cable.

Mountains

The world's highest mountains are in a mountain range called the Himalayas. This mountain range is located in southern Asia. It lies in the countries

Mountain climbers sometimes use ice axes to help them climb up icy or snowy surfaces.

The Matterhorn's steep sides make it difficult to climb.

of Nepal, China, India, Pakistan, and Bhutan. The world's top climbers test their skills in this mountain range. Mount Everest is located in the Himalayas.

The Karakoram range is near the Himalayas in India and Pakistan. K2 is located in this range. K2 is the world's second highest mountain. Its peak is 28,250 feet (8,611 meters) high.

In North America, experienced climbers can test their skills on Alaska's Mount McKinley and Washington's Mount Rainier. Mount McKinley is North America's highest peak. It stands 20,320 feet (6,194 meters) high. This mountain sometimes is called Denali. Mount Rainier stands 14,410 feet (4,392 meters) high. Experienced climbers also may climb Mount Logan. This is Canada's highest mountain. Mount Logan's peak is 19,850 feet (6,050 meters) high.

Mountain climbers sometimes climb in the Alps. This mountain range is located in the European countries of France, Germany, Italy, Switzerland, and Austria. The 15,771-foot (4,807-meter) Mont Blanc is the highest peak in the Alps. But the Matterhorn is the Alps' most famous mountain. Its peak is 14,692 feet (4,478 meters) high. The Matterhorn is very steep. Its sides form the shape of a pyramid. This makes it difficult to climb. Many people have died trying to climb the Matterhorn.

Chapter 2

Famous Firsts

The recorded history of mountain climbing began in the 1500s. Shepherds living near the Alps sometimes climbed mountains to follow their sheep. These shepherds attached spikes to their boots to prevent them from slipping. They also carried long wooden poles to help them balance.

People began climbing mountains for sport in the 1800s. Some wealthy Europeans took vacations to the Alps to climb mountains. These climbers attached nails to their boots and used ice axes.

One of the first famous climbs occurred in 1865. An English explorer named Edward Whymper and six other people climbed the

Early climbers carried poles to help them keep their balance.

Matterhorn. On July 14, they became the first people to stand on the mountain's summit. But four of Whymper's team members fell and died as they descended the mountain.

By the late 1800s, climbers had reached all the Alps' major peaks. Climbers then began traveling around the world to find other challenging mountains to climb.

George Mallory

In the early 1900s, the goal of many climbers was to reach Mount Everest's summit. Several British teams tried to climb it in the 1920s. In 1924, George Mallory led a team up Mount Everest. Mallory had tried and failed to climb Mount Everest two years before.

On June 4, 1924, two members of Mallory's team began the final and most difficult part of the climb. Edward Norton and Theodore Somervell climbed to within 900 feet (274 meters) of Mount Everest's summit. This was the highest anyone had ever climbed. The two men then turned back because they could not breathe well enough to continue.

Edward Whymper led the first team of climbers up the Matterhorn.

Team members pulled Maurice Herzog on a sled after he became severely frostbitten.

Mallory and team member Andrew Irvine made one last attempt to reach the summit on the morning of June 8. Team member Noel Odell watched them climb from base camp. Odell last saw Mallory and Irvine at 12:50 p.m. A heavy mist then moved over the mountain. Mallory and Irvine never came down. No one knew how far Mallory and Irvine had climbed until 75 years later. In 1999, a team of climbers found Mallory's body less than 1,000 feet (300 meters) from the summit.

Maurice Herzog

Until 1950, no climbers had ever reached a mountain summit higher than 8,000 meters (26,246 feet). That year, a French climbing team led by Maurice Herzog attempted to climb Annapurna. This mountain is located in the Himalayas. Annapurna's peak is 26,545 feet (8,091 meters) high. It is the 10th highest mountain in the world.

Herzog's team experienced great difficulties on their expedition. They faced storms and strong winds. Many team members suffered severe frostbite. Herzog later lost all of his fingers and toes due to frostbite. But on June 3, Herzog and team member Louis Lachenal reached Annapurna's summit. In 1952, Herzog wrote a book about his adventures titled *Annapurna*.

Junko Tabei

In 1953, Hillary and Norgay became the first men to stand atop Mount Everest. But a woman did not stand on the summit until more than 20 years later.

A Japanese climber named Junko Tabei wanted to be the first woman to reach Mount Everest's summit. In 1975, Tabei led a team of 14 women about 21,000 feet (6,400 meters) up the mountain. They set up tents there to rest. But then the women heard a crashing sound. It was an avalanche. The women were buried in the rushing snow.

Tabei became unconscious after the avalanche. When she awoke, she found that all her companions were still alive. Later, a group of Sherpas rescued the group. Sherpas are people who live near Mount Everest in eastern Nepal. They often guide climbers on the mountain. The avalanche did not change

Junko Tabei has climbed many of the world's highest mountains.

Tabei's mind. She wanted to finish her climb. On May 16, she achieved her goal. Tabei became the first woman to reach Mount Everest's summit.

Chapter 3

Modern Climbers

By the mid-1960s, climbers had reached the summits of almost all of the world's tallest mountains. But climbers still set records and make important climbs today.

Reinhold Messner

During the 1980s, several climbers were attempting to climb all 14 mountains that measure 8,000 meters (26,246 feet) or more. An Italian named Reinhold Messner was one of these climbers. Polish climber Jerzy Kukuczka and Swiss climber Marcel Ruedi also wanted to achieve this feat.

Messner climbed his first of the 14 mountains in 1970. He and his brother

Mountain climbers still make challenging climbs today.

Reinhold Messner was first to climb all the world's mountains that are taller than 8,000 meters (26,246 feet).

Gunther climbed Nanga Parbat. This Himalayan mountain is 26,658 feet (8,125 meters) high. The two brothers suffered severe frostbite during their climb down the mountain. Gunther became lost and died in an avalanche.

Messner continued climbing after his difficulties on Nanga Parbat. In 1975, Messner climbed Gasherbrum I in the Karakoram range.

In 1978, he and Peter Habeler climbed Mount Everest. They were the first climbers to reach the summit without using oxygen tanks. Messner climbed K2 in 1979. He climbed Himalayan mountain Shisha Pangma in 1981. This mountain is 26,398 feet (8,046 meters) high. In 1982, Messner reached three more of the 14 peaks. He climbed four more of these mountains between 1983 and 1986.

In 1986, Messner climbed Himalayan mountains Makalu and Lhotse. Makalu is 27,766 feet (8,463 meters) high. Lhotse is 27,890 feet (8,501 meters) high. These were Messner's final two mountains. He had accomplished his goal.

Tomo Cesen

During the 1980s, a Yugoslavian climber named Tomo Cesen completed climbs many people thought were impossible. Cesen often climbed solo.

Cesen became famous among mountain climbers in 1985. That year, he climbed three mountains in the Alps in only four days.

The mountains were the Eiger, the Grandes Jorasses, and the Matterhorn.

In 1989, Cesen climbed the Himalayan mountain Jannu in about 23.5 hours. This mountain is 25,289 feet (7,708 meters) high. Jannu also is called Kumbhakarna. No one had ever climbed a mountain of that height so quickly.

Cesen made his greatest climb in 1990. No one had ever climbed the south face of Lhotse. Lhotse is very steep. Many other climbers had tried to reach its summit from this side and failed. Messner called the climb "a problem for the year 2000." But Cesen climbed the south face solo in only two days. Today, many climbers call it one of the greatest climbs in history. But some climbers doubt Cesen ever reached the summit. He had no witnesses or photo evidence to prove his achievement.

The south face of Lhotse is very steep.

Millennium Climb

In 1999, Pete Athans led a team up Mount Everest to take a new and exact measure of the mountain's height. This expedition was called the "Millennium Climb."

Athans and his team climbed Mount Everest slowly. They used four camps along the way. They spent several nights in each camp. They sometimes climbed down to a lower camp. This helped their bodies become used to the high altitudes. They then were more prepared for the final part of the climb.

Athans led the team to the summit on May 5. Team members used a Global Positioning System (GPS) to measure Mount Everest's exact altitude. This small electronic tool uses a group of satellites in space to track object positions and locations. The team found that Mount Everest stands 29,035 feet (8,850 meters) high. This is 7 feet (2.1 meters) higher than previously thought.

The World's Highest Mountains

Mountain	Height		First to Summit
	Feet	**Meters**	
1. Everest	29,035	8,850	Edmund Hillary, Tenzing Norgay
2. K2	28,250	8,611	Achille Compagnoni, Lino Lacedelli
3. Kangchenjunga	28,169	8,586	George Band, Joe Brown
4. Lhotse	27,890	8,501	Fritz Luchsinger, Ernst Reiss
5. Makalu	27,766	8,463	Jean Couzy, Lionel Terray
6. Choy Oyu	26,906	8,201	Herbert Tichy, Sepp Jöchler, Pasang Dawa Lama
7. Dhaulagiri	26,795	8,167	Albin Schelbert, Ernst Forrer, Kurt Diemberger, Peter Diener, Nima Dorje, Nawang Dorje
8. Manaslu	26,781	8,163	Toshio Imanishi, Gyalzen Norbu
9. Nanga Parbat	26,658	8,125	Hermann Buhl
10. Annapurna	26,545	8,091	Maurice Herzog, Louis Lachenal

Climbing Disasters

Mountain climbing is dangerous. Climbers die on mountains every year. They may lose fingers and toes to frostbite. They also may suffer serious injuries during falls.

Climbing groups keep records of climbing accidents. Each year, the American Alpine Club and the Alpine Club of Canada publish a report. This report summarizes information about known climbing accidents in North America that year. Climbers read this report to learn about other climbers' mistakes. This helps them avoid making similar mistakes.

The Mount Everest Disaster
In 1996, Scott Fischer and Rob Hall were expedition guides on Mount Everest. They

Mountain climbers must use the proper equipment to prevent accidents.

led groups of less experienced climbers up the mountain. Both were skilled guides and climbers.

In early May, Fischer and Hall led an expedition up Mount Everest. Many climbers believe May is the best month to climb the mountain. Severe storms are uncommon in May. The expedition members reached Mount Everest's summit on the morning of May 10. They saw clouds below them when they looked down.

A severe snowstorm soon hit the mountain. By late afternoon, winds blew at speeds of 75 miles (121 kilometers) per hour. The wind was loud. The climbers had to shout just to hear one another. The snowfall was thick. The climbers could not see more than a few steps ahead of them.

Temperatures grew colder as the storm continued. The climbers huddled together for warmth. Some of the climbers were able to continue down the mountain and reach the safety of camps. Other people at the camps rescued climbers trapped at higher altitudes.

Lene Gammelgaard and Scott Fischer were on Mount Everest on May 10, 1996.

But eight climbers died on the mountain. Fischer and Hall were among the dead.

Jon Krakauer was one of the surviving climbers. Krakauer wrote a book about the events on Mount Everest that day. The book's title is *Into Thin Air: A Personal Account of the Mount Everest Disaster.*

The 1995 K2 Disaster

In 1995, Alison Hargreaves of Great Britain became one of the world's most famous female climbers. In May, she climbed Mount Everest solo without using extra oxygen. No woman had ever achieved this before.

Hargreaves' goal was to climb the world's three highest mountains. In August 1995, she joined an expedition to climb K2. On August 13, Hargreaves and her team of six climbers reached the summit. They arrived late in the day. They had to climb down in the dark.

A severe and unexpected storm hit K2 less than 2 hours later. Winds on the mountain reached speeds of 100 miles (161 kilometers) per hour. Hargreaves and one of her team members never made it back down.

No one is sure exactly what killed the two climbers. At first, many people guessed that they were caught in an avalanche. But climbers later found Hargreaves' body about 4,000 feet (1,200 meters) below the summit. She had fallen a long distance. Some people believe the strong winds blew her off the face of the mountain.

Alison Hargreaves died as she climbed down K2 in 1995.

Mountain Climbing Today

Climbers have completed many of the world's most difficult climbs. But challenges still remain. Some climbers attempt new and difficult routes that no one has ever climbed. Others try to set records for climbing speed. Some climbers try to climb as many mountains as they can in a set amount of time.

Climbers also challenge themselves by climbing groups of mountains. For example, they may try to reach the summit of the highest mountain in each continent. These mountains are known as the "Seven Summits." Some climbers try to reach the summits of the highest mountains in Canada. Others try to complete the Grand Slam

Climbers may try to climb difficult routes up mountains.

of Colorado. Climbers achieve this by climbing all 54 of Colorado's mountains that are higher than 14,000 feet (4,267 meters).

Technology

Today's climbers can use technology to climb faster and more safely. Climbers use computers to plan expeditions. They may track weather conditions on the Internet. For example, they keep track of the direction storms are heading. Climbers also may use computers to estimate the amount of supplies they will need.

Climbers sometimes bring GPS units to a mountain's summit. Climbers then can find out the exact height of the mountain.

Protecting the Environment

Climbers must take care of the environment. In the past, many climbers left their trash behind on mountains. Over time, many mountains such as Mount Everest became littered with trash. Trash can be a danger to climbers and wildlife. It may block climbers' paths. Animals may eat trash and become sick.

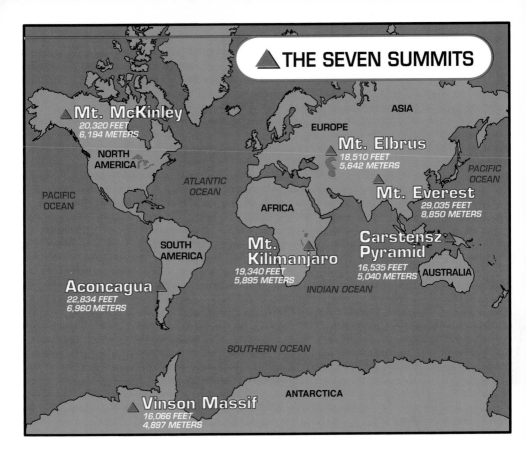

▲ THE SEVEN SUMMITS

ASIA

EUROPE

Mt. McKinley
20,320 FEET
6,194 METERS

NORTH
AMERICA

Mt. Elbrus
18,510 FEET
5,642 METERS

ATLANTIC
OCEAN

PACIFIC
OCEAN

Mt. Everest
29,035 FEET
8,850 METERS

PACIFIC
OCEAN

AFRICA

SOUTH
AMERICA

Mt. Kilimanjaro
19,340 FEET
5,895 METERS

Carstensz Pyramid
16,535 FEET
5,040 METERS

AUSTRALIA

Aconcagua
22,834 FEET
6,960 METERS

INDIAN OCEAN

SOUTHERN OCEAN

Vinson Massif
16,066 FEET
4,897 METERS

ANTARCTICA

Many of today's climbers pack their trash instead of leaving it behind. Some climbers pick up trash they find along the way. They may even form climbing groups to clean mountains. These climbers want to keep the mountains clean for future generations of climbers to enjoy.

Words to Know

altitude sickness (AL-ti-tood SIK-niss)—a condition that occurs at high altitudes when the body does not obtain enough oxygen

avalanche (AV-uh-lanch)—a large mass of ice, snow, or earth that suddenly moves down the side of a mountain

crampon (KRAM-pon)—a metal spike that attaches to a climber's boots with straps; climbers use crampons to walk on snow and ice.

expedition (ek-spuh-DISH-uhn)—a long journey made for a special purpose

frostbite (FRAWST-bite)—a condition that occurs when cold temperatures freeze skin

hypothermia (hye-puh-THUR-mee-uh)—a condition that occurs when a person's body temperature becomes too low

summit (SUHM-it)—the highest point of a mountain

To Learn More

Armentrout, David. *Climbing.* Outdoor Adventures.Vero Beach, Fla.: Rourke, 1998.

Jenkins, Steve. *The Top of the World: Climbing Mount Everest.* Boston: Houghton Mifflin, 1999.

McLoone, Margo. *Women Explorers of the Mountains.* Capstone Short Biographies. Mankato, Minn.: Capstone Books, 2000.

Platt, Richard. *Everest.* Discoveries. New York: D K Publishing, 2000.

Useful Addresses

The Alpine Club of Canada
Indian Flats Road
P.O. Box 8040
Canmore, AB T1W 2T8
Canada

The American Alpine Club
710 Tenth Street
Suite 100
Golden, CO 80401

Himalayan Explorers Club
P.O. Box 3665
Boulder, CO 80307-3665

Internet Sites

The Alpine Club of Canada (ACC)
http://www.alpineclubofcanada.ca/index.html

The American Alpine Club (AAC)
http://www.americanalpineclub.org

Get Lost Adventure Magazine
http://users.itsnet.com/home/getlost/
    mountain.html

Himalayan Explorers Club
http://www.hec.org

MountainZone.com—Climbing
http://www.mountainzone.com/climbing

Index